OTHER LOVERS

JACKIE KAY

Other Lovers

BLOODAXE BOOKS

ISBN: 1 85224 253 1

First published 1993 by
Bloodaxe Books Ltd,
P.O. Box 1SN,
Newcastle upon Tyne NE99 1SN.

Bloodaxe Books Ltd acknowledges
the financial assistance of Northern Arts.

Cover printing by J. Thomson Colour Printers Ltd, Glasgow.

Printed in Great Britain by
Bell & Bain Limited, Glasgow, Scotland.

Acknowledgements

Some of these poems were broadcast in the BBC 2 *Words on Film* series in *Twice Through The Heart*, a poetry documentary based on the life of Amelia Rossiter. Others have been broadcast on *Poetry Please*, *With Great Pleasure* and *Stanza*. Acknowledgements are also due to the editors of the following publications in which some of these poems first appeared: *Blue Nose Poetry Anthology* (1993), *Critical Quarterly*, *Of Eros and of Dust* (Oscars Press, 1993), *Poetry Review*, *The Popular Front of Contemporary Poetry* (Apples and Snakes, 1992), *Scotland on Sunday* and *Sixty Women Poets* (Bloodaxe Books, 1993). Some of these poems were dramatised in *Every Bit of It*, a play about Bessie Smith produced by the Sphinx Theatre in 1992. 'The Year of the Letter' was commissioned by Bookworks as part of a library project.

I wish to thank the Arts Council of Great Britain for awarding me a Writer's Bursary for 1993.

Contents

Even the trees

Even the trees outside feel it, their fine branches
their sixth sense of mercy,

they bend into the wind and ask for forgiveness
to come in a storm,

and join the congregation of silence; that tall witness.
One man, tied to a tree and whipped

never worked again in the cotton fields. In the early
light, the delicate bone-light

that broke hearts, a song swept from field to field;
a woman's memory paced centuries,

down and down, a blue song in the beat of her heart,
in an old car that crossed

a railroad track; the scream of a warning –
is that why we remember certain things and not others;

the sound of the bass, the sound of the whip, the strange
strangled wind, bruises floating through light air

like leaves and landing, landing, here; this place.
Everything that's happened once could happen again.

In the Pullman

Bessie and I are in her Pullman heading for Tennessee.
Bessie and I are in her Pullman heading for Tennessee.
We got so much heartbreak, we can't divide it easily.
I take one piece, she takes another, we both drive
And our sadness drives further,
It's way up ahead, ahead of Bessie and me.

And even in the springtime it's hanging from the pawpaw tree.
The road is long and flat, the fields are repeating the cotton.
The road is so long and flat. Life is like that.
We drive without moving. We try and carry on, but
There's this big sadness hanging from the pawpaw tree.
It's way up ahead, ahead of Bessie and me.

The Right Season

They followed the tobacco crops in the spring,
the cotton crops in the fall, all along the flat plains.
It had to be the right time, the right town,
where for the blues, people had enough money to spend.

Call it a blues trail. A trail that led to a big tent.
Town after town, people packed in like rice in a bowl.
On she would come, the Empress, the Voodoo Queen.
Blast the blues into them so people remembered who they'd been.

Took them to the sad place. The place they were scared to go.
Took them to the mean place where they knew they'd been low.
Somebody was waiting. And it might have felt like home.
Somebody knew them; somebody could see right into their soul.

And she took them in feathers and plumes,
she took them there in extraordinary costumes;
a wig of horsehair and a lampshade fringe.
Her blues were like secrets, or shocking bits of news.

Travelling on the underground railroad,
out of the tent, a voice faster than the wind.
Where to meet. Which house was safe. Which church.
Carrying the blues from Chattanooga to Chicago.

The tobacco crops in the spring; cotton in the fall.

The Same Note

Every note she sang, she bent her voice to her will;
her voice was a wood instrument or a wind one,
her voice had the power to turn the sails of the windmill,
or knock down a tree with the force of a hurricane.
She could get it right back like some kind of boomerang.
She could use it as a shelter, the roof of her mouth,
stopping the rain, stopping the rain soon as she sang.
Or she could fly out of Alabama, or float the mouth
of the Mississippi Delta. Or walk the solid flat plain.
She could tell every story she wanted to tell;
and pass them on through the new towns, across the mountain.
Her voice could bring people running, like the church bell
could when it was used as a warning. And then again,
if she wanted, she could rock herself to sleep, to dream.
Her own cradle swinging the same note, again and again.
The same note. The solid flat plain. Exactly the same
note, like the church bell, could bring people running,
could tell them she'd been in their heaven or hell.
Every note she sang, she bent her voice to her will.

The Red Graveyard

There are some stones that open in the night like flowers
Down in the red graveyard where Bessie haunts her lovers.
There are stones that shake and weep in the heart of night
Down in the red graveyard where Bessie haunts her lovers.

Why do I remember the blues?
I am five or six or seven in the back garden;
the window is wide open;
her voice is slow motion through the heavy summer air.
Jelly roll. Kitchen man. Sausage roll. Frying pan.

Inside the house where I used to be myself,
her voice claims the rooms. In the best room even,
something has changed the shape of my silence.
Why do I remember her voice and not my own mother's?
Why do I remember the blues?

My mother's voice. What was it like?
A flat stone for skitting. An old rock.
Long long grass. Asphalt. Wind. Hail.
Cotton. Linen. Salt. Treacle.
I think it was a peach.
I heard it down to the ribbed stone.

I am coming down the stairs in my father's house.
I am five or six or seven. There is fat thick wallpaper
I always caress, bumping flower into flower.
She is singing. (Did they play anyone else ever?)
My father's feet tap a shiny beat on the floor.

Christ, my father says, that's some voice she's got.
I pick up the record cover. And now. This is slow motion.
My hand swoops, glides, swoops again.
I pick up the cover and my fingers are all over her face.
Her black face. Her magnificent black face.
That's some voice. His shoes dancing on the floor.

There are some stones that open in the night like flowers
Down in the red graveyard where Bessie haunts her lovers.
There are stones that shake and weep in the heart of night
Down in the red graveyard where Bessie haunts her lovers.

Blues

Hell, I can't even take my own advice,
that's what she thought often, when her left eye
(always the left) was swollen and a blue river
ran underneath the brown; or when
whole parts of her body could not
be walked on, or swam in, or touched even.
When her body had no-go areas; something-only areas.
Danger: a fence right round her skin, wooden
as her own voice the morning after

all that violence. It was in the way they looked at her.
It was not in her mind. She did not grow such looks
in her own backyard. The hard stare; the furtive one where
the eyes were a fast car swerving as she walked near.
Nothing could persuade her not to be funny.
She could not stop being funny. Making people
laugh till they cried, hurt themselves, howl.
She was a shouter. She could barrelhouse.
But on the morning after all that violence

she could not raise the roof of her voice.
She could not embellish or endow or growl.
Laugh, yes. Grunt. Giggle. Once she caught herself
in the trembling mirror. *A minstrel.*
She tried to be completely still.
As if she were committing a murder.
A clown. An aunt jemima. She has a smile
that could cross a river. And she had a laugh
that could build a raft. And that was all she had.

Twelve Bar Bessie

See that day, Lord, did you hear what happened then.
A nine o'clock shadow always chases the sun.
And in the thick heavy air came the Ku Klux Klan
To the tent where the Queen was about to sing her song.

They were going to pull the Blues Tent down.
Going to move the Queen out of the town.
Take her twelve bar beat and squash it into the ground.
She tried to get her Prop Boys together, and they got scared.

She tried to get the Prop Boys together, and they got scared.
She said Boys, Boys, get those men out of here.
But they ran away and left the Empress on her own.
She went up to the men who had masks over their head

With her hand on her hips she cursed and she hollered,
'I'll get the whole damn lot of you out of here now
If I have to. You are as good as dead.
You just pick up the sheets and run. Go on.'

That's what she done. Her voice was cast-iron.
You should have seen them. You should have seen them.
Those masks made of sheets from somebody's bed.
Those masks flying over their heads. Flapping.

They was flapping like some strange bird migrating.
Some bird that smelt danger in the air, a blue song.
And flew. Fast. Out of the small mid western town.
To the sound of black hands clapping.

And the Empress saying, 'And as for you' to the ones who did nothing.

Watching People Sing

Carrie Carrie Anna. My mum's away.
Gie it laldy. Gie it laldy.
Our room shifts and tips axis
crashes towards her jaw
dropped, slack and quivering.
Closes the eyes. Dreams the song.

I am old enough to do the buffet.
Pass a bit of this, a bit of that.
When Alec sings *Ae fond kiss*
his soft lips part like petals.
He is another life away.
Someone's with him. *Ae fareweel.*

I grow up with party social.
Dress for it in two-inch platforms.
The chorus sways on the couch;
banners with big words. *For a' that.*
The mouths of the people of the past.
Everyone has their way of singing.

Peter's chin, doing its dinger,
judders, hings on to the last note –
a massive electric shock. *Put your sweet
lips a little closer to the
flooooooooooooooorrr.* Margaret's conceded
after the tenth *come on Margaret*

g'on yoursel hen. She sings and smokes
Any old time you want to come back home.
Her man replies *It's a quarter to three* in a semi-
American accent learnt in the Glasgow Odeon.
I can't sing. All I can do is watch
and clap, and clap, and clap.

My dad's up now for the rest
of the night. Songs like roll calls.
Far away in the hills of Croft-amie
Smoke dances across, swish, swish
in its soft skirts, moves me to tears,
the salt of songs – *where the white man*

fears to tre-ad. He throws his head
back for the high note coming
in like a keen north wind *there's a*
dah de-de dah de-de DAH DAH DAH
Come on John. Another song.
The shirt's unbuttoned. Centre stage.

The farthest I've climbed in a windie SILL
The wee cigar held, a conductor's baton.
I'm the bar room mountaineeeeeeer.
Betty Toner upstages him; smooth dance
across the blue ice-rink, she glides
and turns *sing me a song of Bonnie Scotland.*

Her voice is a pattern on the floor.
Any old song will do. Everybody claps
in time. *Take it away Betty.*
The music swirls out the chimney.
The whole house trembles and remembers,
songs with the wrong words, the right sentiment

a heavy scent behind our ears.
People are what they've been in this room.
A good dancer. A patter merchant. *What a night, eh?*
How many. Nights with the same songs
growing on the skin like hairs. I am
sixteen. I blow-dry my mother's hair.

Too old for this really, I move
between glasses, topping up
the Teacher's whisky. Yet still, Anna's voice
singing *John Anderson my Jo John*
makes the song mine. I know him.
I can see him coming down the hill.

Now we maun totter down John
And hand in hand we'll go
And sleep thegither at the foot.
Oh God, I think, Oh God, who will
sleep at my foot, who will sing to me like that
eyes brimming with love and change and spark.

Sound

Inside the fast world
I do things for myself.
Inside the fast world
I translate motion into sound.
An underground train makes my body shake
and I create the din it makes,
coming into the stations.

Today a car suddenly stopped.
A child opened its mouth wide.
And three birds rose at the same time;
their feathers synchronising.
A police car arrived flashing lights.
Screaming into the spring;
the blossom, impossibly still.

The noises of the past
float into my room at night.
The icecream van's mad jingle;
a street full of children shouting.
High pitched voices in the wind.
The bell of an old till; the drawer's spring.
A big ball bouncing, bouncing.

Inside the fast world,
my hands talk to themselves at night.
In my head, the water tank babbles
incoherent language. There is
the small cough of a house in the dark.
There is the feather weight of my cover.
Inside my head I am full of light.

Sign

They did not see
the way she talked
as language. It was
a handshape. A movement. Located
in the wrong place at the wrong point
in time. That each symbol
was a sign was not thought
possible; *no language at all*

no tongue

When she talks,
she uses space: a room,
a field, an ocean. Her words,
a camera lens; everything she sees,
she hears, zooming
in to the
sound of a black-eyed susan,
and out
to span a wide-angle; the clearances, fossils, folksongs.

things far away

things close-up, she sees
it all *(no language at all)*
in the present tense: a flashback
is something held between her thumb
and her index finger, faster
than memory, or film.
It is this

vast linguistic space,
this intricate grammar, growing
as a fish grows its fin, a foetus
its eyelashes. Nothing is
learnt. Everything grows
in the right place.

Imagine

seeing language in shapes
before your eyes – dynamic
and metrical – forcing
you to focus;
your conversation a spatial relation-
ship between mouth, eyes and hands.
The space between the planets.
And somebody telling you, *that's miming*
that's pantomime. Somebody who
cannot separate a word
from a thought.
All this

distance

between one language and another, one
culture and another; one religion
and another. The *little languages*
squashed, stamped upon, cleared out
to make way
for the big one, better tongue.
These things happen
between

time

The day they forced her to speak
their tongue, she lost
the black-eyed susan.
She went back in
time

They say her voice is very strange.
They tie her hands behind her back.
They say repeat after me until
she has *no language at all.*

Gastarbeiter

When she moved to the new country
the trees were tall strangers,
the light was the colour of metal
and the air was diesel
(although her words for these
were different)

till she learned the new tongue
and spoke it like a faltering step
wanting to please, *thank you,*
nervous, crossing the road, eyes
full of apologies, *excuse me please,*
walking, quick, quick, to work

a sharp needle, the long swathes
of material, long enough to wrap
twice around the dead; a close family.
The noise of the machine jabbering
as the same cloth came back to her for
another stitch, the end of the story.

In a narrow house with her small
children, she finished a fairytale
she liked so well, poverty,
teaching herself new words; Hansel, Gretel.
At night her dreams were huge uninvited guests,
folding white wraps for small children.

In one bed they all slept, rolled
tight, a bandage on an open wound,
gaster, bite her; sleep is always light
when stars are the shapes of swastikas
and the limbs of hate move clockwise.
Late, late tonight she will hear

a soft terrifying sound, something
will fall through the furious mouth.
She will gather her children up in her arms
and jump as the house goes up, swearing
behind her, where the grandmother, mother
daughter, *Tochter*, will be ghosts in another room.

In my country

walking by the waters
down where an honest river
shakes hands with the sea,
a woman passed round me
in a slow watchful circle,
as if I were a superstition;

or the worst dregs of her imagination,
so when she finally spoke
her words spliced into bars
of an old wheel. A segment of air.
Where do you come from?
'Here,' I said, 'Here. These parts.'

Compound Fracture

That day
after the bone came through my skin –
my mother's voice split open

right into my ear, saying my name,
and then saying her own, on a phone not there;
not herself, using a strange tone.

It is her. I screamed for her, desperate.
She was in the next room repeating our names
until the nurse

burst into the white casualty
her eyes bulging with cruelty; a terse –
Now Now Now, her voice hailstones

pelting – *You won't be seeing your mother
unless you button
that thick lip*, and worse, worse.

So walls come in.
I tried to fasten
every button along my bottom lip, down to my

poisoned apple. I realised what
the nurse had said only by looking
at her body and her lips:

the starched white
of her uniform; her tight fitting
mouth; her polished black shoes. Whips.

That sardonic tongue; that regiment cap.
My mother was still in another world, taking sips
of sweet tea for shock; I ached for her soft lips.

Colouring In

When you go back, nothing is real.
You search car after car for somebody familiar,
but strangers rest their satin hands,
when the light is red, at the Cross.
You'd settle for someone you didn't like.
Eileen Mackie with the yellow buck teeth.

The old primary school is a toy model;
it has a grey gate you can open and close.
None of these children makes you believe
it happened – no Chinese ropes or skipping songs.
You are always seeking a girl
whose name has been changed

from Brown to Green, who had a passion
for ballroom dancing. When she came home
to yours, your father moved the living-room
armchairs, threw her inbetween his legs.
Nobody even looks like her any more.
Her with the Red Admiral mouth.

There used to be a hairdressers there
where you sat for hours under a huge helmet.
(Some big girl always peeped in and said,
'No ready yet,' and your head burned.)
Next door: a dentist where once you tried
to jump through the window after the gas.

You could fill the gap, know where you are,
if you could smell the cobbler's leather.
On this new road, all the protests have flattened out-
American style, with drive-in *Texas*.
The same garish red and yellow in every town,
selling the same home to the same person.

You want the voice of somebody real.
Somebody who would shout for the UCS.
But even the struggles seem fairytales.
The Party was in the parlour counting Moscow gold.
Somebody else has the key to your locker.
All you remember is your burning hands, after

a day's hard, mad sledging; the way you stood
by a genuine fire, worried about chilblains
and getting old. It is still the same house
with a different fire, imitation coal;
flames you now turn down by number.
This winter your mother had a change of heart.

Later, you drive off alone to your place.
Your father says, 'Where did you go? Fintry.
How did I know. You are so predictable.'
But only the hills, only the Fintry hills
the early evening light skipping
across them like a wee girl with a big rope,

the faraway rhyme of a song you used to know,
the empty yellow stretch of land.
Only the hills where you definitely remember
having an egg, a painted face of an egg,
rolling it down, all the way down, to the bottom,
where it did smash, it did, and you were happy, you were.

Keeping Orchids

The orchids my mother gave me when we first met
are still alive, twelve days later. Although

some of the buds remain closed as secrets.
Twice since I carried them back, like a baby in a shawl,

from her train station to mine, then home. Twice
since then the whole glass carafe has crashed

falling over, unprovoked, soaking my chest of drawers.
All the broken waters. I have rearranged

the upset orchids with troubled hands. Even after
that the closed ones did not open out. The skin

shut like an eye in the dark; the closed lid.
Twelve days later, my mother's hands are all I have.

Her face is fading fast. Even her voice rushes
through a tunnel the other way from home.

I close my eyes and try to remember exactly:
a paisley pattern scarf, a brooch, a navy coat.

A digital watch her daughter was wearing when she died.
Now they hang their heads,

and suddenly grow old – the proof of meeting. Still,
her hands, awkward and hard to hold

fold and unfold a green carrier bag as she tells
the story of her life. Compressed. Airtight.

A sad square, then a crumpled shape. A bag of tricks.
Her secret life – a hidden album, a box of love letters.

A door opens and closes. Time is outside waiting.
I catch the draught in my winter room.

Airlocks keep the cold air out.
Boiling water makes flowers live longer. So does

cutting the stems with a sharp knife.

Fridge

In the cold room there is tomorrow:
the red floor to clean,
and a brand new broom.

Your father's body is lying flat out –
the white ledge inside the clean fridge.
Rigid. Serene.

Imagining always starts with death, then
dances the world. A second in a window,
that man, that's him!

It's been done before:
names, letters, photographs.
An ice cube inside your neck.

The fear of turning back.
In the fridge he is the colour of negatives;
he is not in the ballroom, dancing.

You clean the mortuary.
In and out the pail of disinfectant.
The strange smell behind your eyes.

Footsteps vanish. Red tiles shine.
Only the cold breath of the dead in this room.
What was it he might have said?

Nigeria was hot red dust; did he go back?
Then this black man is a stranger.
You are not his.

Somebody else's then. You should not look.
Pull open the fridge panel, frightened.
Kiss the cold lips.

Tough

You know what happens to you
when you start to think like that:
your whole house is upside down;
the radio's on; it's the man's news
in that voice (that sleek, oiled Mercedes voice).
He upsets you; and your speakers hang in a void.
You climb out your window like a thief.
You grass on yourself. You breathe too fast.
The roof's fine point is nailing the pavement.
How come everyone's else chimney reaches for the sky?
Them across the street are not playing ball
with your wee boy. So you bring him in
through the upside-down window.
The BFG is talking in a funny voice
about children's dreams in jars.
So all you need to do is pick up a paper
and head instinctively for this headline:
GAY SUICIDE IN THE ISLE OF MAN
You're like that; you can't kid me on.
The voice going *sick ill sick.*
I understand. Don't give me who am I to understand.
Right. Just because I'm not you.
Things happened to me too. Times
we didn't know if the next meal was coming
from a win on the National or a neighbour's bowl.
You're not the only one who's had it tough.
It's absolutely your own paranoia:
Backlash. Crap. Videos in your bathroom – nonsense.
You don't need to say anything.
I'm right inside your head.

The Day

This is the day when everything (not just some things) goes wrong.
I go out and my back tyre's deflated; an off-key song.

Both lights in my bedroom blow like sudden sorrow.
In the kitchen the ceiling's just gone yellow.

My bed collapses. My sheets rip. Outside it is thunder.
The dogs, wild next door, are asking for murder.

Bastards. I go to get a beer from a wet fridge, and I swear
I see something dart across the floor; my own fear.

It *moves* incredibly fast. Everything has been peculiar
since the moment I heard. My skin is pale beyond belief.
Is this to be it then? Thumping the pillow. Alone. Grief.

Therapy

In the city, that summer, she craved
the cold stone of churches, those buildings
full of empty wooden pews, the smell of musk.
She wondered what the man, who was going
off his head, would make of her, kneeling, whispering.
Her head bowed like a broken flower.
Or the woman who asked to be sectioned.
If she could see her now in the morning
of the stone summer, trying to remember
an old psalm, or a childhood prayer. Easter.
Green hills. Zuleika. Zuleika. Her own name
strange to herself on the stone floor.
Her own name, a string of beads, a rosary;
even a confession. The summer of stone.
She was the sane one supposedly,
the one who said, *what comes to mind,*
as they lay on the couch. She was the one
stroking the 14th century floor, deep-
breathing that strange erotic smell.
Watching the tall glorious candles burn.

This Long Night

This long night talks to itself.
The dark won't listen to the sound of your name.
I reach out here – my big empty bed.
The space next to me closes in; you say something,
anything, the exact sound of your accent
falling like rain on a caravan roof.
Tell me what you want me to do.

This long night stretches into another time.
Nobody calls my name. Silence –
a thief in the back garden.
Your body, a shadow, flat under the moon.
In my sleep, I open up like a night flower.
My scent comes in the midnight hour.
You come in by the window, don't you?

This long night and I can't reach you.
Your tongue inside me slides away.
You walk till the night grabs you.
A lonely pitch at the dark. Walk
until the road is all of your past.
Then, turn in your sleep next to your marriage,
wake yourself up calling my name.

B

The Keeper

Nowadays there are too many things to hide.
I am a keeper. Secrets are my caged animals.
I feed them things. Things they will like.
Each day, a ritual; I keep time, though

there are days when I wish I could say,
to Hell and watch the entire city run
riot with hippopotamus and rhinoceros.
A city gent, an autobank, an elephant.

She has told me not to tell anyone.
I don't. These lies are fun. I'm good at them.
Not since I said my brother drowned
have I told such a whopper. One lie

leads to another: a zebra on the escalator.
There's a monkey swinging on Waterloo bridge.
Your face high up, till I pull you down.
London bridge is falling down, falling down.

I am losing it. I count time on fingers.
Another hour when I can't see straight.
The zebra is coming down with no stripes.
Somebody's messed with the zebra's stripes.

I wake to the sound of your voice
moving around my hollow head, my empty house.
I imagine your house. What colour are the walls?
The sheets? You and she, asleep between them.

Are they stripes? I picture you in this bed.
Here, my home. Nobody knows. I behave oddly.
The two lions stayed in their bed of hay.
I thought that awful funny –

the cage wide open. Soon it will out;
the truth always does. What will I do then?
Capture them in a net of lies.
One day I will keep things from you.

Dusting the Phone

I am spending my time imagining the worst that could happen.
I know this is not a good idea, and that being in love, I could be
spending my time going over the best that has been happening.

The phone rings heralding some disaster. Sirens.
Or it doesn't ring which also means disaster. Sirens.
In which case, who would ring me to tell? Nobody knows.

The future is a long gloved hand. An empty cup.
A marriage. A full house. One night per week
in stranger's white sheets. Forget tomorrow,

You say, don't mention love. I try. It doesn't work.
I assault the postman for a letter. I look for flowers.
I go over and over our times together, re-read them.

This very second I am waiting on the phone.
Silver service. I polish it. I dress for it.
I'll give it extra in return for your call.

Infuriatingly, it sends me hoaxes, wrong numbers;
or worse, calls from boring people. Your voice
disappears into my lonely cotton sheets.

I am trapped in it. I can't move. I want you.
All the time. This is awful – only a photo.
Come on, damn you, ring me. Or else. What?

I don't know what.

The Crossing

I

That evening, walking across the bridge,
the light drowning in the river,
the dark water wringing its hands,
till the bridge moved too, that evening.

And you, my love, were not there.
We did not walk together to the small room
where your hands floated across sheets;
daylight behind the curtains.

Suddenly, in that dark place, I felt myself
go to you; as if I were two and one of me
went to you.

The bed, a boat on a dangerous crossing.
Neither of us knew where we were going.

II

The river is drowning its hands.
You are not here this evening.
I am crossing the same bridge alone.
Underneath it is dark and fast, the river.

I can't see myself. Lights hang on trees
by the banks – glowing and forbidden.
Dropping like fruit into the dark water,
only to rise again.

No matter how many times we try to sink
our past – old bundles of clothes in the river –
the body surfaces

suddenly, covered in wreaths. You are not there.
Someday you might go back. Love is light and dark.

III

I am looking for the same small room.
Perhaps you are in it waiting.
Would you take me in and feed me.
Whisper the talk of the river, babble tongue.

Having all leads to nothing. There's the bundle
of past going down the river where one bank
becomes another. Now you have gone back.
I am here, crossing over, returning home.

It is my turn to drown memories.
Your face reflecting the strange evening light
at the top of a hill, looking down on red roofs.

Your eyes wistful, wanting it all back.
It is my turn to miss, to look in the river.

Away from You

This isn't a memory. It is something I am doing.
Something I always do when I am not with you.
I repeat everything; and it happens to me again.
You pull down the zip of my jacket. Kiss me.
Especially, in this place, in this weather.
The rain shining the big slabs of stone
outside the old mill house. The trapped hill
opposite moves like a large animal in heat.
I walk across its back; while you get into a red car
in a foreign town. It is probably raining there.
Splashing you, as the door opens for you.
I lose you in the traffic. I panic.
Your car crashes. I am at your funeral.
There's the long low wail of the organ.
I see my own death happen before my eyes.
I am in this other place, waiting. This is longing.
Going on. Your voice lodged inside my head.

No. You are in the house in the foreign town.
Looking out of the window. I have seen that look
on your face. You have that look on your face.
Now. I climb the stairs slowly to the bed,
the first bed, and you, waking, take me.
Outside the rain runs across the animal's aching back.
Later, in your time, the rain leaves the dusty town.

Other Lovers

1 *What was it you said again there by the river*

And later, when the young danced to an old song,
the moon split in two, the stars smashed,
what was it again?

By the river, by the procession of trees,
the shadow marching across your face,
how deep do you feel?

I hold the light between us. Kiss you
hard in the dark. Ahead of us, the bright blue eyes of sheep.
Are there words for this? Words that sink to the bottom

of the river where ducks flap their sudden wings,
startle silence; believe me, believe me.
We walk this night, shining our bright eye ahead.
Do you love me, love me, do you.

2 *The Day You Change*

The lace curtains go up.
She starts saying *you always say*;
you realise you always do.
On the living wall, strange shapes spread
like those on hospital sheets.

She closes the curtain round herself;
you hold your hand against the side of your cheek.
Tonight, you eat an instant meal
(no long spaghetti, no candles.)
Conversation limited

to *pass the pepper.* In the bedroom
the cover is stretched taut,
pulled back and forth in a battle,
till the small hours leaves one of you cold.
How long is a night like this?

3 *When you move out*

You mark each box with a thick black pen.
You will always be neat, no matter what's said.
And fair. You do not pack what is not yours.
Even the joint presents: the Chinese vase,
the white dinner plates, the samovar,
you leave to her. You won't miss things.

At night you will lie on a different side.
Listen to another station to send you to sleep.
You will never play Nina Simone, again.
Other things won't be possible. Restaurants,
parks, cinemas, pubs. Avoid them. They are dangerous.
Never go near another garden. There's no point,

growing peonies to blossom without you. Delphiniums.
Take up something else. *It doesn't matter what.*

4 *Swim*

So, at the end of a perfect rainbow
you have upped and left, and I
have taken to swimming a hundred
lengths of breast-stroke per day.
This is the way of love.
Even swimming, I am obsessed
with the way your feet arc
when stroked, your legs,
the long length of them,
how I could have you all worked
up in seconds. My fingers
doing the butterfly, you saying,
Don't stop Don't stop Don't stop.

5 *She never thought she could with anyone else*

And now, here she is, whispering urgently into another ear.
Holding someone else tight. After the sixth month,
she returns the *I love you*, she's heard since day one.
In your island she lies in the sun like a traitor.
But you are always standing on her shoulders.
She starts to do things the way you did them.
She stacks dishes in order of size.

She begins to like your favourite cheese.
In restaurants she chooses the wine you chose.
She finds herself getting irritated
at the way her new lover makes a bed.
She misses smooth corners, no creases.
She scrubs the bath twice a day, and at night,
sees the wrong lover mouthing her name.

6 *Worse than that*

One day you find you are your other lover.
You use exactly the same expressions,
like a child uses its mothers.
You disapprove of the same things. Refuse
to laugh at certain jokes. Uncertain
of yourself now, you start to imitate an absence.
You don't know what to think of the News.
Your world lacks gravity. Her presence.
You drop yourself from a height. Don't fall.
You are scared to go from A to B
– she was the map-reader.
You're scared of new things to eat.
You poke at them on your plate, depressed.
Long for your favourite meal, a simple life;

until you learn to cook on your own
and it's good (though you say it yourself).
Out and about, you are so confident
you're taking short cuts, back alleys,
winding your way past yourself,
up a narrow cobbled close into the big High Street.
You stand, looking down, the air bursting
through your raincoat like a big balloon.
You manage to fathom one of those machines. *Easy.*
Catch your slick tenners, *No bother,*
and saunter off, whistling to yourself.

You have actually done it.
You would never have believed it.
You have a whole new life.

Full Moon

Out with you tonight, I followed your eyes to the sky
and started to sweat. I knew what I was in for.
I tried to pull your hand out of your pocket,
but it wasn't budging. So I rushed you home,
seeking shelter in bed where a window
of light is our old movie, flickering on the wall
opposite: two men with their back to us watch
the crazy sea; or clouds rush by like rounded-up sheep
in the land above the moon.

You wake me in the middle of the night:
Do you love me? Truthfully. How many others.
What did they kiss like. What did you write
to them. 'I want you; did you write I want you.'
I try to soften your body, make our sleeping spoon,
but it will not bend, and I am not the man who bends spoons.
On the wall, the men reel in the past
on a strong line. Every full moon, it is the same:
the taste of an old song.

I drifted back, dreamt of a dead girlfriend
who was up and running. You shook me, *You never smiled*
in your sleep. You can't love me any more.
I went under cover to perform a self-examination.
Way above it grins its goat-cheese grin.
The day before it expands to a complete ball, your hands
start knitting at nothing, grow fine wool hairs.
Your eyes widen till every question you've ever asked
swims in them, those round pools.

I hold out my untrusted hand against the tide.
But you are a swine that wants killed; a tree whose wish
is to warm rooms. If I ever forget why
I soon see it, high above, wreaking havoc,
full of itself, till later, it splits a fat side, laughing.
Then, relaxed, we go kissing down stairs. Out in a fine
wind, we set sail. Safe, until the next time when I sing,
What a little moonlight can do to you.
And you scratch yourself till blood comes.

A Country Walk

In the dark afternoon light, we two walk
in the soft insistent rain, along the country road,
between two massive hedges no one can see over.

At the turn of the bend is the baby you long for:
a red head, a girl, her two small feet
running ahead of us. You are coming to her

a long way off. And the rain is harder,
soaking us right through. She calls
in the strange light; the sky a slate, wordless.

You fear her, me, our future. Suddenly
five magpies split in the sky like atoms.
The fields lose their boundaries.

The hedgerow gone. The smell of cowdung.
The black earth split open. She still waits.
Who is her father? Which country is her home?

All this is harder than the rain; us two together.
Than the dry stone dyke which guards the farm.
Or the grey sky that reveals no secret. No one

can tell us the way; we are miles off. At the turn
of the bend, a fairytale house stands, innocent.
Carved in stone. You could have that room;

I could have the east. We could both grow things.
Inside the small holiday house, we eat the bricks.
You light the fire. We sit in tender silence.

Only, your face is raw, thinking, thinking;
your eyes sweep the floor into the corner.
Your tongue is a silent poker stirring the fire.

Snap

In this light, your lips open
like a red flower; a sparkler in your hair.
Strange things always happen for our love.
We watch deer dance towards us in red light
far above the city. We go to speak the same word.

In this light, the graveyard is haunting, beautiful.
The gold trees guard the stones like faithful dogs.
We start to say we wouldn't mind being buried here:
till the barn owl sings its one note
on the gloved hand of an Irish man.

The Year of the Letter

LETTERS

In the morning of the New Year
you wrote a bitter letter to an old lover.

A while later, you watch a huge ball bluiter
the local library. The man is miles away
on a steel ladder to the sky;
he sweats and sweats like January rain.

Your face is coarse wool as you deal
a slanting furious hand, *answer me*.

Inside your church, not hers, the old smell.
Candles and the sweet musk of praying.
Down the road a woman sniffs her crisp fivers

which appear like God through a hole in the wall.
Today the air is thin and smells of recession.
You lick cold metal from a lamppost.

A hundred books flap their pages like broken wings.
Everywhere is a sign: TO LET CLOSING DOWN.
The big ball swings again; again.

IN

The doors opened early and for one hundred and three years
the public had come in winter or summer, early or late,
wearing coats or jackets or hats to read the newspaper,
discover a family illness, or borrow a book for bed,
search the name of a rare flower,

or seek a book about a big bear who got lost, only
what was the name of the author?
To look up the Parish Register (Burials 1559-1883)
or find the telephone number of an old lover,
sit (unfit) in the Reference Room
reading *The Encyclopaedia of Swimming*
or sleep through *The Waking Dream.*

In and out she took the books, stamped with red ink dates.
Sometimes when she liked somebody she read everything.
From when she was a child. The smell of books.
The smell of silence.

I never go to the children's section,
all they've got is little women –
Heidi and Rapunzel, Anne of Green Gables,
when what I want is Lady Chatterley, Madame Bovary,
Hedda Gabler, Anna Karenina.
I always say, 'THESE are for my parents'
and use their cards (they never use them)
and that librarian with the cow-lick fringe
just blushes, stamps the book, no questions.

She found a relative in the Directory of Crematoria.
She found a novelist she would die for.
She learnt by heart the definition of claustrophobia.
She recited names in the local census (1881-1891) like incantations.
The M-Mortuary Drawer in Local History was a fatal obsession.
The syllabus for a course she never took lay in Universities, Box 7.
She looked tentatively into her family history, they were all mad
            as hatters.
She lived in The Book of Saints, especially the Seven Sleepers:
They were walled in a cave, the seven youths of Ephesus under
            Decius
(250) and were found alive in the time of Theodosius
(362). Saints all seemed to be called Catherine or Agnes.
The Furniture Beetle is closely related to the Deathwatch Beetle
from the Anobiidae family. Latterly she preferred beetles to people.
They could make quite lethal holes even in wood that is brittle.

BIOGRAPHY

She fell in love. Her heart opened and flapped
like so many pages in the wind. Everyday she got higher.
Smiling at the people bent over papers.
Grinning at the swots and the surreptitious
who scooped knowledge up in heavy armfuls,
and never shared it, nor said what they were doing.
Smiled at those who anxious, pulled out one book
then put it back and pulled out another.

My father caught me at it one day.
Radclyffe Hall dropped out from inside Bunty.
Page 106 was enough for him; he frog-marched me
down to the library where Cow Lick stammered,
'I thought it was for you,'
and my father disturbed the silence:
'What is the matter with you?' inbetween tight teeth.
My skin clung to my white blouse, innocence.
It was so hot, so hot. I nearly passed out.

She was in love. There was no turning back.
She took her letters to the library and read them
in between her book, so that she could read her lover
like a book, and get a thrill. A shiver
sung like wind through barley up and down her back.

'Darling,' they began in the middle
of A Glossary of Wood, 'I want you.'
Something in the silence named it.
She wrote back, her pen scratching and screaming,
'I'm wild about you, the slap and fetch of you.
You are my world, you know that don't you.'

REFERENCE

You have seen the man on the crane before. Haven't you.
Isn't he the man who went to school with you.
Primary Four. Who later was in this library
every morning scouring the Job Pages.
Now he is up there. Can he smell himself?
What does it feel like?

AND

Even as a child she preferred books to people.
Her own family called her anti-social.

My father never trusted a person who liked books.
He said BOOKISH like a bad word.
And, 'you'll turn yer brains to oil
wey a' that reading.'

But here was a place set apart for books.
A place where people went and did not pay.
And here was a lover who took her in her arms at night
and left her mark, who knew her by the look of her cover,
who whispered poetry to send her under,

Down we go my love, down, down.

RECENT HISTORY

One day she left you for someone else.
Left poetry and stories she'd written to amuse you.
Left the Bach and the Pergolesi
that you had to return to the local library.
Left her Middlemarch and her new leggings,
her toothbrush and the Encyclopaedia Britannica
a Bette Davis film (which could have been a warning)
and your heart in sharp splinters of glass or wood,
your heart like a stuck cassette exploding in your hands
curls   thick wool
ribbons   Figures of 8
*   circles*
*   hate playing*
out
the old 40s
*   movies*
smoke, dice, fire.

Y

All she could do was ask a question.
These library doors flew open in 1890.
Now the wings of the building are about to be crushed.
The loose neck of the spire, strangled.
So what she remembers (absurdly)
is hearing her grandmother say:
'Hen. Go down to the leebrary and get a book to read to me.'
Because her grandmother couldn't read.

She stands watching books, carried out in coffins.
Until some thing, like a branch inside her long
throat, snaps into a furious song:
Where have all the flowers gone? We shall overcome.
The answer is blowing in the wind. Some day ay ay ay.
I'd hammer out a warning. Get up stand up. Babylon.
Her voice strung high as the steeple, bellowing.
The people from the market across the road join.
The man comes down from the crane.
The woman in her church comes out from confession.
A young girl stops licking her ice cream to sing.
This is fantasy. Nothing happens. She does nothing.
But watch it go. The big filthy ball swing.

The page closes. You never receive a reply
to that letter so different from the days of darling.
Yesterday, you passed a woman who punched numbers furiously
into a wall and never got anything.

Going to See *King Lear*

On the big red smooth seat, I
watch the giant television
and my mother's eyes, greedy,
gulping everything down like
chocolate raisins. In front
of me are rows of heads that
put me in such a bad mood:

sleek shining page-boy, snobby
at the back; tight bossy bun,
trapped in a net; tall, selfish
beehive blocking my view. Then,
all of a sudden, darkness
comes down, sweet, and will not melt
in the hand or in the mouth.

I am sitting with strangers,
just the shapes and silhouettes
of them now. We breath in, all
of us, in one breath waiting
to be changed, to stop time or
for the trailer to end and
King Lear begin. No children,

except me, watching with mum,
who leans forward, her body,
diagonal, her fury
at good King Lear's disloyal
daughters, she whispers, 'Get out'
to the good one. Or 'Don't put
up with that.' (I think it was

Cordelia.) When King Lear's
Gloucester gets his eyes gouged out,
my mother falls off her chair.
I cover my eyes. Too late.
I've seen it. The terrible
tormenting sight of a man's
hands over his helpless, scooped

sockets, staggering back to
some other time of trust, whilst
those egg-whites of his eyes run.
'Vile jelly,' I shake, appalled.
Lear foams, whisked-white, at the mouth.
Jesus, my mother says, shocked,
That was good. That was so good.

Her eyes glint, green with pleasure.
Deep sigh when the names appear
and disappear. So slowly,
she rises from the red seat.
I had to see it. I did.
What a good, good girl, sitting
all quiet. My mouth has fallen

open for good. It won't close.
I am seven. I have seen
Lear's best friend get his eyes poked
out. The red floor is sliding
downwards. I will fall into
myself years later; grown-up,
velvet curtains drawn open.

Pork Pies

We're not together any more.
After Bobby Baxter followed us home,
drank our pop and ate our mini pork pies
(he had five) our whole life

changed. We kept him in our room
upstairs; taught him our special tongue,
watched him flash up on television.
Missing three days, four days, six, seven.

On the last day at ninety degrees Fahrenheit,
Robert James Baxter looked out our high window
and waved. He had been warned. Bad Bobby.
And some ugly nosy Parker looked

up, some pain-in-the neck village golfer.
Putt Putt Putt. 999. A hole in one.
Next thing: the policemen at our door;
our mum there in her brassière,

the loose language of gin, opening
and closing her mouth; her eyes narrow
and fierce as a bird's; a seagull's fury,
calling us down, calling us down,

Hannah and Helen. Never Helen and Hannah,
we dressed in the same black patent leather
shoes, shining like mirrors. Our checked
gingham dress, its pink and green squares.

Our jet black hair parted in the same centre;
our east-coast identical accents, *well spoken*.
The village plodder held the picture in the air.
'Have you seen this boy?'

'No Sir.' We said together. Pause. 'No Sir.'
Big boys in blue searched our room,
but Bobby Baxter, beautiful Bobby Baxter,
wasn't found till five days later.

Got You

You know I am the shy one really, don't you,
not you; that your maths have my answers,
then how come I am the slow one

and you are the one who shines. School Dux.
Prefect. Your blazer is shabbier than mine
but Gran from Dornock loves you better

than me and so does our mother. The dog
licks you. People who say they can't tell
the difference drive you crazy: your skin is creamier,

your nose less wide; your hair loose floppy
curls, not *frizzy*, not *sheep's wool*. I know,
I know like I know the back of my hand. Last night

in the top bunk, I wanted to climb down
and do something. Can't tell what. Not even in our tongue.
I swallowed hard listening for the sound of real sleep

till I must have given in again.
You know me better than I know you.
Always get me. I sat bolt upright, my heart

flapped like our bedroom curtains, your night-time
laughter, soft, squeezed to your chest, doubled-up:
'Got you. Didn't I. Got you again.'

Condemned Property

My son hit me.
It's my fault my son hit me.
If I had said something else
he wouldn't have, surely.
It's rained all day; thick rain sliding
from the gutter down the bulging wall.
I can't stop. I'm using my sleeve,
mopping myself up like filthy lino.
What kind of mother am I?

I've run my fingers up and down
the bruises on my arm. Soft, tender.
I've looked in the mirror.
My skin is stretched, wide. My eyes. Terrible.
Drive your car into the red brick wall.
I've breathed air through a tiny hole
right at the top of the narrow stairs.
Sucked it, gulped it, and run down.
The builder said this house should be
a condemned property. 'See that crack.'
Cut your fat leg with the black knife.
'The wall is on the move. Could crash
any time. Needs one more inch. A hot summer.'
There is something the matter with my eyes.
They are weeping like drains and changing colour.
What could you have done, what could you?
I talk to myself in this baby-voice
I used to use for my son, *tell Mum.*
To avoid these bruises, gathering clouds,
the unmitigating rain, thrashing down.
More placid, more docile, *you could have been*
more placating – *soothed him, sushhh, sushhh.*
I could have used reason like some use floss.
Bash your head against the bulging wall.
I use it, staring into next door's house,
run the white gloss wire back and forth
between my own teeth till blood runs.

His voice has broken. That's it.
Get it through your thick skull.
I definitely shouldn't have screamed.
And when he knocked me over,
I should not have tried to get up.
Because he wouldn't have had to, then,
knock me over again. *My lovely boy.*

No Way Out

You tie the kitchen towel into a garotte.
There's no way out, no way out.
You hit me with the rolling pin.
There's no way out, no way out.
I notice a steak knife missing.
There's no way out, no way out.

We're too old for this I shout.
There's no way out, no way out.
He just keeps on and on about
there's no way out, no way out –
a fiver, dinner, my brother.
There's no way out, no way out.
He walks towards me, that odd mouth.

I pick up a knife to protect myself.
There's no way out, no way out.
He keeps walking towards me.
There's no way out, no way out.
The knife is smiling. Come on, kill me.
There's no way out, no way out.
He walks towards me, that odd mouth.

Love

For the first time in my life I had a love-child,
planned like a garden, wanted. I swelled
with pleasure, passing days along the coast,
light breeze, laughing. I was forty, laughing.

We stared at simple things, fulfilled.
Walked into surprises, open-mouthed, toasted
ourselves. All for us: the fire juggler; the dog passing
by on the roof of the motor car; the half moon.

I never wanted anyone so much so soon.
Desire shook me, pears from a tree, past blossom.
Suddenly something went wrong. Love gone rotten.
Our child screamed through paper-thin nights.

You write notes. We fight. You won't talk.
You write notes. We fight. You won't talk.
The walls come in like a terrible tide.
Trapped here, marooned, mouth open wide.

Mouth

Now the lips I love are the ones I hate
at night-time and love again in the morning.

The same mouth that said I love you
holding hands walking this coastline,

the wind blowing our hair into wild partings,
says things you could never imagine.

Words like dead gulls thrown out the sea;
your mouth froths like a drowning man.

How long was it before you wore laughter
behind your belt, whispered whore, whore.

Till I stared at the sea's violence of waves,
every day the stones cutting my walk by the shore.

Inside

Inside I'd say, don't please.
Grit my teeth. Bite the pillow.
You pulled me to the place
where everything went numb, hollow.
I'd lose my voice.
Grit my teeth. Bite the pillow.
Inside I'd say, don't please.
High on the wall, I'd watch your shadow
turn against me – shape of a storm.
My own heart, broken like bones.
I'd wish at night for tomorrow
when I might wash you away and sorrow
would leave me alone, alone.
Nothing washed you away.
You, underneath my skin.
That smell, that voice, that hollow.
My own heart, broken like bones.

China Cup

This china cup, every night, this china cup.
The same fragile bone china from home.
My hands cupping bluebells. Locked in.

In my cell, I lift my mouth to my china cup.
The same fragile bone china from home.
Outside, the long stretch of stone. Tide in.

Every night, this hot drink from my china cup
in this small cell like the one at home.
Four walls here, four there. Tide in.

Every night, this same routine – china cup,
powdered milk. Alone. Sipping away at home.
The noise of the key turning. Locked in.

Landslide

His body is buried in the land.
You are buried here: this place
where your voice is

a disused mine. You mime
the same sentence. The sound gets stuck.
Life. Life.

You wait for the time that never comes.
Days slide into nights, waiting.
Nights long like years in a small room.

You learn to speak from your stomach.
Your voice box lies in the ocean.
The sea's bed is softer than this one.

The wind sings through cells.
You buried something and forgot
where you put it. Years ago.

Maybe you even forgot what you buried.
How it went. What the tune was.
Remembering is dying slowly.

Every night, a heaviness spreads
over thin, inadequate sheets, violates,
sharp, sudden, staying till morning.

Till the unlocking when Cleopatra comes
with her big keys and lets you out.
You wash, but the smell comes back

again. Again, a song's refrain.
Dying is remembering slowly.
Slipping away. Walking the same

coastline until your body steps
like land slides into the sea –
under the path people will later walk over.

Finger

What is it made of? Guilt. Blame. Sometimes,
as if pain demands I point a finger –
one of the terminal members of my hand.

This instrument; this fine tune. Listen.
I know which notes will strike a chord.
I use my fingers as a measure.

Like the pointed sheaths of a reaping machine;
the bit the knife comes through to cut corn.
Simply: flesh, blood, marrow, bone?

There is no room for conversation; no other questions
to ask. Nothing to do, but say: That was wrong.
How big was the slave's room?

Have you been to the plantation? Tobacco. Sugar.
The quarters – the temperature of a hot house. Plants.
The placing of plants in a soil so they may grow.

Breeding in the dead heat of a tiny room for the master.
Or him groping you as your man stands by.
And him fingering the money.

And me, a songster, marking music, the strange colour
I will play soon in the wooden holes. Plantation.
The skin growing on trees. Listen.

Watch the way my fingers move across your temple.
Answer me. They say it doesn't exist anymore.
This is another century. Take my fingerprint.